The Little Book of

RANGERS

Edited by
NEIL CAMERON

CARLTON
BOOKS

This edition published 2008
First published by Carlton Books 2004

A CIP catalogue record for this book is available
from the British Library.

ISBN 978 1 84442 574 7

Printed in Singapore

INTRODUCTION

Rangers Football Club is not like any other club, it's an institution. And sometimes the team can make you want to be locked away in one, such is the roller-coaster ride they put their fans through.

Most people don't get a choice over whether or not to support Rangers. You are just born into a family that goes to Ibrox every week. No arguments. End of story.

With more than 100 major trophies to their name, Rangers can claim to be the most successful club in the world and, if that isn't enough, they have legends such as McCoist, Baxter and Laudrup to boast about too.

In over 135 years of history Rangers have provided enough thrills, spills and heartache to fill the plot-lines of even the most outrageous soap opera. But as many people in this book point out, they wouldn't go through so much drama for anyone else.

❝Ibrox really is a special place. It's incredible the bond fans have with parts of the ground. They can remember the day Baxter passed from here or there, and from where Gazza scored. I remember at training spotting little burnt areas. These were from people who had sneaked in at night and sprinkled the ashes of former fans on the pitch.❞

Sandy Jardine, *who made 674 appearances between 1965 and 1982*

❝That development will remain a monument to the club's forefathers who believed that only the best was good enough for Rangers.❞

*Club historian **David Mason** on the rebuilt Ibrox stadium which was completed in 1929 with Archibald Leitch's magnificent grandstand as centre-piece*

"Though The Streets Be Broad Or Narrow, Then Follow We Will, We Will Follow In The Footsteps Of Our Team. Follow Follow, We Will Follow Rangers, Everywhere, Anywhere, We Will Follow On, Dundee, Hamilton, even up to Aberdeen, Should They Go To Dublin We Will Follow On."

'Follow Follow', the Rangers fans' anthem

‘The bad news for Scottish football is this is as bad as it gets for Glasgow Rangers.’

Walter Smith *after the 1998 Scottish Cup Final loss to Hearts. Rangers won a Treble the following season*

❝I only ever have a drink when we win a trophy. That's why people think I'm an alcoholic.**❞**

*Midfielder **Iain Ferguson***

❛What do I like about Rangers?
I like winning.**❜**

Mark Hateley *after scoring a goal on his return to Rangers in 1997*

"A wonderful club when you're winning. A tough old club when you're not."

Richard Gough, *1997*

Just walking through those doors every day was an absolute pleasure.

Dave McKellor, *former Hamilton goalkeeper who spent a year at Ibrox*

❝I would walk across broken glass for that club.❞

*Striker **John Spencer** on Rangers*

"I remember the date as if it were yesterday: Monday, October 30, 2000. The day Dick Advocaat tried to rip my heart out."

Lorenzo Amoruso *opens his autobiography with memories of the day the Rangers captaincy was taken off him*

'I told them I didn't collect losers' medals and threw it away. I think a couple of kids fought over who would get it.'

Graeme Souness *treats his runners-up Scottish Cup medal from 1989 with disgust*

❝At Rangers, you are not as good as your last game. You are as good as your last pass.**❞**

Richard Gough

> **"Nine out of Ten. Must Do Better."**

Slogan on advertising boards a year after Rangers' famous nine championships in a row when they were selling a new home strip

‟ He took his curiosity to extremes: it was not unknown for Struth to carry out simple surgical procedures himself on terrified footballers laid out on the dressing-room table at Ibrox. ”

*Journalist **Alex Murphy** on long-lasting manager Bill Struth who won 18 titles, 10 Scottish Cups and two League Cups between 1920 and 1954*

❛Take it, but make sure you put it back one day.**❜**

*What **Bill Struth** told fans who wanted to take a blade of grass from the hallowed Ibrox turf*

❝I have never seen a player run a Rangers side ragged like that ever before in my life.**❞**

Scot Symon, *manager from 1954 to 1967, on Jim Baxter, two months before signing him from Raith Rovers*

❝There were times when Jim Baxter seemed to be on a different planet. He really was that good.**❞**

Denis Law

❝ Are you not ashamed to be on the same pitch as me? **❞**

Jim Baxter *to Alan Ball during the Wembley game of 1967 when Scotland were crowned 'unofficial World Champions' after beating England 3–2*

❝I was going to score an own goal, just to say I'd got a hat-trick at Wembley. Then Denis Law, who had played in the 9–3 game, told me that he would kill me if I did that.❞

Jim Baxter, *who scored both of Scotland's goals in a 2–0 win over England in 1962*

❝I knew that it was time to retire when there were players beating me that I wouldn't have peed down in the past.**❞**

Genius **'Slim' Jim Baxter** *reflecting on the end of his playing career*

'The greatest player I have ever seen.'

Willie Thornton *on Jim Baxter*

'The Ledge.'

What everyone at Ibrox calls the legendary John Greig, once voted the Greatest Ranger of All Time. Greig made 496 appearances between 1962 and 1978 and was manager from 1978 to 1983

'Greigy hit me once. I got up and then a moment later I was down again. Then seconds after that he dumped me on the track at Ibrox. I said to him, "John, are you trying to intimidate me?"'

*Celtic winger **Jimmy 'Jinky' Johnstone** on how they played in the old days*

> **❝**I was lying in bed on a Saturday morning, reading the paper, when my phone went. The caller was Rangers director, Jack Gillespie, and he offered me the manager's job at Ibrox. I was flattered but declined with thanks. John Greig was a good friend of mine and I had no intention of being involved in ousting him.**❞**

Sir Alex Ferguson *from his autobiography,*
Managing My Life

❛I feel that it's a great privilege
that the club still allows me
to work here.**❜**

John Greig *on his role in the PR office at Ibrox*

❛Everyone injured was to receive a visit from a player or an official and the club was to be represented at every funeral. If an injured fan had a favourite player and word got back to Ibrox, Mr Waddell would make sure that player made a personal visit. No one could say Rangers didn't respond to the tragedy. Willie Waddell was magnificent.❜

Sandy Jardine *on the Ibrox disaster of 1971 when 66 fans died*

"I still think about those people every single day of my life.**"**

John Greig *on the victims of the Ibrox disaster*

'The Wee Blue Devil.'

The nickname of brilliant 1920s winger
Alan Morton

❛Other than getting a couple of blokes with balaclavas to beat him up, I have no idea how to cope with Brian Laudrup.**❜**

Hibs boss **Jim Duffy** *on the Danish star who lit up Ibrox*

❝He will never play for
Rangers again.**❞**

Words alleged to have been uttered by manager
Walter Smith *about Peter van Vossen after the*
Dutch international missed an open goal
in an Old Firm game

❝I knew that even if I had scored a hat-trick in every game I still wouldn't have got a game.**❞**

*Striker **Kenny Miller** on his unhappy time at Ibrox under Dick Advocaat*

“I would honestly play them every single week.**”**

Ally McCoist *on games against Celtic*

❝I got so excited before the game that I started to hyperventilate. They got me to breathe into a bread bag just to get me right again.**❞**

John Brown *on his Old Firm debut*

'For every £5 Celtic spend, we will spend £10.'

*Chairman **David Murray** with a quote which came back to haunt him*

"We're signing Paul Gascoigne. "

Walter Smith *ends a press conference with a bombshell in 1995 after Celtic had just won an Old Firm game 3–0*

❝You can put on my gravestone
that Andy Goram broke
my heart.**❞**

*Celtic manager **Tommy Burns** after a typically
brilliant performance from the Ibrox goalkeeper*

> I never want Celtic to win anything, but if they had to win the league as they did in 1998 then I wish Tommy Burns had been in charge. He is a really nice guy.

Andy Goram

> **❝**I phoned Tommy Burns afterwards to explain my point of view. We had a 40-minute talk about the game and my respect for the man just grew.**❞**

Iain Ferguson *after the 'Nine in a Row' Old Firm game in which he and Celtic's Paolo Di Canio had to be separated*

❛It was my first-ever game against Celtic and Tommy Burns kept giving me encouragement, saying that I was having a good match and to keep it going. I couldn't believe it!❜

Derek Ferguson *on unusually sporting behaviour during a Glasgow derby*

❝For my first-ever Old Firm game I was actually in the Celtic End. Henrik Larsson got me a ticket.**❞**

Giovanni van Bronckhorst *on life before Ibrox*

Everyone knows he is a crazy Celtic fan.

Lorenzo Amoruso *after a spat with Ayr United's James Grady*

It literally ruined my whole summer. We'd had a great season but all I could think about was that final.

John Brown *on the 1989 Scottish Cup Final defeat by Celtic which denied him a Treble*

'The gaffer, Graeme Souness, stopped me on the stair and asked me where I was going with the trophy. I just wanted to get close to the fans. '

Terry Butcher *on the 1987 League Cup win over Celtic*

'Happy New Year, Bhoys.'

Ally McCoist's *response to Celtic players who were unhappy with the way he went down for a penalty in the first game of the year*

❝Whenever I'm
In Times Of Trouble,
Mother Mary Comes To Me
Singing Glasgow Celtic 1, Caley 3.
Celtic 1, Caley 3
Celtic 1, Caley 3
Glasgow Celtic 1, Caley 3.**❞**

*Rangers fans rejoice in their old rivals' misfortune
to the tune of 'Let It Be'*

'He's a fantastic player. When he isn't drunk.**'**

Brian Laudrup *on Paul Gascoigne*

'Everyone thought Brian was clean-living. You should have seen him crawling along the hotel corridor, drunk, while on pre-season tour.'

John Brown *reveals how Laudrup was initiated into Rangers*

❝I always said that a team who drinks together, wins together.**❞**

Richard Gough

' Richard Gough is one of the best players I ever came up against. He was as good as Willie Miller and I can't give a bigger compliment than that. **'**

Charlie Nicholas

"What can I say about Ally,
I love him.**"**

Jorg Albertz *on Ally McCoist*

❝ I was welcomed to Ibrox by McCoist and Durrant spraying Ralgex all over my underpants. **❞**

Iain Ferguson *on fun and japes in the dressing room*

'And the winner is... oh, it's me again.'

Ally McCoist *handing out the BBC Sportscene Personality of the Year award*

He had the fattest backside in football at the time.

Walter Smith *hails a 'not quite fully fit' McCoist
after he scored the winner in the 1993
League Cup Final*

'Police officer: "Mr McCoist, do you have a police record."

Ian Durrant: "'Walking on the Moon'…"'

*From **Ian Durrant's** autobiography, **Blue and White Dynamite***

I'll play professional football as long as I can. Then spend the rest of my life being depressed.

Ally McCoist

' And here is Ally McCoist to break me record and he does. I hate him. **'**

Derek Johnstone *watching Ally score his 133rd league goal for the club*

‟He does look as if he can replace me. He's only got about 300 goals to go.„

Ally McCoist *on new signing Erik Bo Anderson who scored twice on his debut*

Sorry, Mr Chairman, but this is the earliest I have been late for some time.

Ally McCoist, *who was famous for his poor timekeeping, to a bemused and impatient David Murray*

❝I told McCoist that the chairman had never been late for his work in his entire life, yet he was an hour late this morning.**❞**

Walter Smith *after McCoist and David Murray had shared a bottle of wine over contract talks*

'Jock brought me into his office and said there had been a bid for me. I told him I wanted to stay and still think he was trying to see what I was made of.**'**

Ally McCoist *on the managerial wiles of Jock Wallace*

We played Hearts and got beat 2–0. Every one of us owes big Jock an apology for that day.

Ally McCoist *on Jock Wallace's last season as Rangers boss*

❛No comment, lads – and that's off the record.**❜**

Ally McCoist *to a group of reporters during a club media ban*

❝Even now when I'm asked for my autograph, I wonder if they were one of those who booed me.**❞**

Ally McCoist *remembers the not so good times at Rangers during his first stint with the club*

‘You can't live in Glasgow and be called Nigel. He's going to be Rab.’

Ally McCoist *on the arrival of Nigel Spackman*

"I don't like being called Kevin."

Kevin 'Ted' McMinn

‘The Italians are known for that, boss. Fowl play.’

Ally McCoist *after Graeme Souness warned his players that the Italians once tried to poison Trevor Francis' chicken dinner*

❝Ally was good enough to phone my wife and tell her that I wasn't too badly injured. I asked him what she said and his reply was: "Trevor, she can't believe I'm not playing."❞

Trevor Steven *on McCoist's help when he was stretchered off during an Old Firm game*

❝ I looked at Gary McAllister and he looked at me as if to say, "I can't believe this noise." **❞**

Ally McCoist *on the Leeds United game at Ibrox in 1992*

'Ladies and gentlemen of the jury… Oh, that was last week.**'**

Ally McCoist *at a supporters' do, a week after a brush with the law following an 'incident' outside an East Kilbride pub*

‘Ally turned to me and said,
"I usually score from here."
And he bloody did. ’

Alex McLeish

‘Why did I push him out on the pitch to take a bow? Well, it belongs to him.’

Dick Advocaat *on Ally McCoist, then with Kilmarnock, on his last appearance at Ibrox*

> **❝**I never played for Rangers. There was a cripple and a catholic in front of me.**❞**

*Former Scotland manager **Craig Brown** is modest (and not very PC) about his time at Ibrox*

❝I spent the last 10 minutes constantly asking the referee to blow for full time. I had nothing left.**❞**

John Greig *on the 1972 European Cup-Winners' Cup win over Dynamo Moscow*

❝I was presented with the trophy in an ante-room in the bowels of the Nou Camp. You could say it was an anti-climax.**❞**

John Greig *on the presentation of the cup after the pitch was invaded by ecstatic Rangers fans*

❝The Spanish police did what was natural to them. The Rangers fans did what came naturally to them and charged.**❞**

Jock Wallace *on the pitch invasion in Barcelona in 1972*

❛My Fellow Bears…❜

Alex McLeish, *then Motherwell boss, addresses
a Rangers function*

> ❝You must allow enough time to savour something that is so fantastic. It is like a woman – the longer you wait for one, the more you appreciate it. Every four years is fine.❞

*Goalkeeper **Lionel Charbonnier** rejects the idea that the World Cup be played every two years*

❝I don't know what I'll do next. Maybe become the next Rangers manager.**❞**

Graeme Souness *in a television documentary in 1986. A month later he was…*

Scottish football is full of hammer-throwers.

Graeme Souness *after new signing Oleg Kuznetzov was injured*

❝As I walked off the pitch all I could see was my dad in the stand with his head in his hands.❞

Graeme Souness *expresses his remorse at being sent off on his debut for Rangers at Easter Road in August 1986*

❝I won't be fining players for getting sent off.❞

Graeme Souness *shortly after his sending-off*

❛I think Graeme had it in his mind that he had to sign a catholic.**❜**

David Murray *on Souness and Mo Johnston*

❝Footballers should not play golf.**❞**

Graeme Souness *who now, of course, plays golf*

❝When Ally scored I looked across to Graeme and he didn't react in any way.**❞**

David Murray *on Souness after the out-of-favour McCoist got the winner against Aberdeen in the last minute*

'I have told Graeme that he has made the biggest mistake of his life. **'**

David Murray *on Souness leaving for Liverpool in 1991*

" I just knew they would win the Scottish Cup the year after I left. **"**

Graeme Souness *on the trophy he never won*

❝I have come to the conclusion that nice men don't make good football managers.**❞**

Graeme Souness

'The best signing I ever made at Rangers was Walter Smith.'

Graeme Souness *on his more than useful assistant manager*

> **'**If you ask me, Walter's been the manager here for the past four years. **'**

Richard Gough *on Walter Smith's appointment in the wake of Graeme Souness' shock departure to Liverpool*

❛Rangers are a big club and I want to win things. They will help me do that.**❜**

Mo Johnston *on his reasons for signing for Rangers from Nantes in July 1989*

‘If I have one regret in my career, it is that I did not join Rangers a lot sooner.’

Ray 'Butch' Wilkins

❛I have to say that I've never had any problems with Trevor's grip.**❜**

Gary Stevens *on rumours that team-mate Trevor Steven had a limp handshake*

'Spurs...'

Alfie Conn *on being asked who he preferred
playing for, Rangers or Celtic*

❛I knew my England career was not going to get off the mark again when manager Graham Taylor kept calling me Tony. That's my dad's name.❜

Mark Hateley

> **‘**That is an awful lot of money to pay for a substitute.**’**

Mark Hateley *on the £4million then record signing of Duncan Ferguson who was supposed to take the Englishman's place in the team in 1993. Hateley won Player of the Year that season*

❝Everyone who knows him will tell you that he's a very pleasant young man and isn't a bad lad at all. He's been guilty sometimes of stupidity, but mostly immaturity. Consider that a young man who is certainly no danger to society is now behind bars with hardened criminals.**❞**

Joe Royle on Duncan Ferguson who 'did time' for headbutting defender John McStay of Raith Rovers in 1994

❝Complaints, moans, complaints. Now listen to this bit: "And you can tell Walter Smith to get his finger out of his arse." And arse is spelt ARSS.❞

David Murray *reads out a supporter's letter to journalists*

> **❝**I never even went into the Blue Room at Ibrox until I had won every medal I could with Rangers.**❞**

John Brown *who waited until he had proved himself before entering Ibrox's 'inner sanctum'*

'John Brown would be in my greatest-ever Rangers team and I make no apologies about that.'

Ally McCoist

Gazza is the perfect house guest. He folds his blanket in the morning. He washed his own cereal bowl. When he first started coming over he was still having the odd cigarette, but always went out on the patio. I thought, "What a polite bloke."

Broadcaster and journalist **Danny Baker**

❝I'll tell you what my real dream is. I mean my absolute number one dream that will mean I die a happy man if it happens. I want to see a UFO. They're real. I don't care if you look at me like that. UFOs are a definite fact and I've got to see one soon.❞

Paul Gascoigne

❝Richard Gough looked at me and asked me to give him one more big effort.**❞**

Paul Gascoigne *on being spurred on to score his wonder solo goal on the day Rangers clinched the league against Aberdeen at Ibrox in 1995–96*

❝If he had said anything to me after the game I would have punched him.**❞**

Andy Goram *on Paul Gascoigne's goal in the 'Auld Enemy' game during Euro 96*

❝Gazza said he was taking his wallet out on the pitch with him. I didn't understand what he was talking about until he told me that he's read something in a paper that my mother said I would either be a footballer or a thief.❞

Marco Negri

❝I remember being in a pub with Gazza and he handed a complete stranger a wad of notes. That's the kind of guy he is.❞

Derek McInnes *on Paul Gascoigne's legendary generosity*

❝Numbers are the thing with me. I have this thing about four. I don't know why four. My favourite used to be five and then seven. Then I got into this thing about 13, where nothing would be done in fours because four and nine are 13. I don't know where nine comes from. I got it into my head because four and nine are 13. That's like six and seven. I can't bear to see them together because that's 13 again. So when I go out on the park I won't go out in sixth, seventh, nor fourth. It will either be fifth or eighth. **❞**

Paul Gascoigne *reveals his compulsive nature*

'There's Only Two Andy Gorams. '

Aberdeen fans to The Goalie who had spoken to the papers about not being 'mentally attuned'

❝The day I had to book Paul Gascoigne for celebrating a goal was the last straw – that was the day I decided to pack it in.**❞**

Former referee **Jim McGillivray** *on the rules imposed on referees*

❝I know why Gazza stays at Rangers. There are two stars in Glasgow: Glasgow Rangers Football Club and Paul Gascoigne.**❞**

Media magnate **Chris Evans**

'Hopefully this will get me back in the good books.'

Gazza *after his penalty wins a game at Pittodrie in 1997. He had just had a public falling-out with girlfriend Sheryl*

‘ Let he who has never had a bust-up with his wife cast the first stone. His private life is his own life. We won't interfere. **’**

*Vice-chairman **Donald Findlay** after Paul Gascoigne's alleged assault on Sheryl*

'I went to Walter Smith and he asked, "Do you like getting in the papers?" I thought for a moment and said, "Not really." And he said, "Well, why do you do it?"'

Paul Gascoigne *on his unfortunate ability to attract publicity wherever he went*

❝Free the Geordie Genius.❞

*A banner held aloft by the Rangers fans who
wanted Paul Gascoigne to stay with the club.
He left two weeks later*

❝My father-in-law is a Celtic fan. I know he shouts at me at the game saying things like, "Fergie, you're a wee so-and-so."❞

Barry Ferguson

'I wasn't up for it. I wasn't sharp enough or quick enough. I just went out there to take it easy but in the first minute I was thinking, "Oh ****, this is not to be my game."'

Fernando Ricksen *on being booked after only 22 minutes of his Old Firm debut*

❝It was a fantastic achievement, made even more special by the fact it was won at Parkhead.**❞**

Donald Findlay *on Rangers winning the Treble at their great rivals' ground*

❝ Jock Wallace told us in no uncertain terms that Celtic had scored two unlucky goals, so we had better go out there and score three bloody good ones. ❞

Davie Cooper *after Rangers had won the Old Firm match 3–2*

'Nothing prepared me for what it was like. It was the greatest footballing experience of my life.**'**

Jorg Albertz *on his first Old Firm game*

One mistake wins the match and the best player on the park made it.

Graeme Souness *on Gary Stevens' underhit back-pass which allowed Joe Miller to win the Scottish Cup for Celtic*

❝I would have loved to sign for Rangers, but I didn't want to be the first catholic.**❞**

Ray Houghton, *who moved to Liverpool instead*

Me and three pals used to jump a wall and play two-a-side on the pitch at Ibrox. I always made sure we shot towards the Celtic End, so I could pretend to score in front of them.

Alex McDonald, *cult hero in midfield during the late-1960s and 1970s*

> I think Jock Wallace made me captain because I knew more verses of "The Sash" than he did.

Jimmy Nicholl

❝ He gave me the runaround. Honestly, I was chasing shadows all day. **❞**

Celtic's **Phil O'Donnell** *on Rangers'*
Trevor Steven

Durranty has just said that he only gets one game a season now and here he has come in and has won us the league.

Richard Gough *after his team-mate scored against Celtic*

‘Finally, when is Andy Goram going to piss off and stop annoying us with his bloody wonder saves? Yours in victimisation,’

*Letter to Celtic fanzine **Not the View***

'These two boys are not the best of players, but at least they help make our team photo a bit more attractive.'

Ian Durrant *introduces Brian Reid and Derek McInnes on a club video*

❝If I had to choose between cricket and football it would be cricket every time.**❞**

Andy Goram *who was also Scotland's wicket-keeper*

❝Don't Worry, Martin. We Don't Want to be Here Either.❞

A banner held up by Rangers fans at Parkhead. Martin O'Neill's days as Celtic boss were rumoured to be coming to an end

In training it was the English versus the Scots. Coisty came in our team because, as I told him at the time, he had played two games for the Sunderland reserves.

Terry Butcher

❝I like rock music. Iain Ferguson is trying to get me into Nirvana at the moment.**❞**

Walter Smith *on his interests outside football*

❝I knew it was time to go when
I walked into the press
conference and wondered
if someone had died.**❞**

Walter Smith *after winning the League Cup
in 1996*

❝I can't say anything. I am annoyed I can't say anything. In every country and every democracy we can say what we want. But they are waiting for me.**❞**

Dick Advocaat *bites his tongue after two of his men were sent off at Tynecastle*

❝ You have to remember that we have our blue noses to go along with the orange shirts. **❞**

Dick Advocaat *after Rangers beat Aberdeen 4–0 in the 2000 Scottish Cup Final when almost every Rangers fan wore a Dutch top*

❝In a game like this we will have to work our sock off. **❞**

Dick Advocaat *shows his command of the English language*

❝We had some new fitness videos delivered in the summer and they were all in Dutch. I couldn't believe it.**❞**

Lorenzo Amoruso

'There are too many big heads
in this squad.'

Dick Advocaat *after a defeat at St Johnstone*

❝There was a story last week that I was leaving in 2002 and had told my friends that. I don't know where it came from. I don't have that many friends.**❞**

*Rangers boss **Dick Advocaat** on speculation linking him with a move away from Ibrox*

❝I know what's gone wrong inside the club and it is quite simple. I know the facts but if I speak about it, I'll have to speak about individuals – and I never do that.**❞**

Dick Advocaat *bites his tongue again*

❝I'm told that when I went to Leicester there was a problem with language. I had given a team talk and later learned that one of the Scots boys in the dressing room was asked by an English lad, "What's a skoosh-case?"❞

Jock Wallace

'I felt their player needed sorted out.**'**

Fernando Ricksen *on his off-the-ball clash with Aberdeen's Darren Young*

❝I'm always having problems
with refs because
I play rough.**❞**

Fernando Ricksen *predicting mayhem. Well, he
did warn us…*

"Oh the Bluebells are Blue."

A song sung at every Rangers game despite the fact nobody knows what it is about

❛Flecky, Flecky, show us yer arse.**❜**

A popular chant for Robert Fleck after he had bared his behind at an Old Firm reserve game

'Putting out a team to play defensively against Rangers at Ibrox would be like sending Salman Rushdie through Tehran on a bicycle.**'**

Aberdeen manager **Ebbe Skovdahl** *responding to criticism of his tactics during the 3–1 defeat at Rangers*

‚He's got more skill than I had when I was five – in fact he probably has more skill than I have now.'

Colin Hendry *on his son Kyle*

Interviewer: "Would you like to be thought of as being as good as Rangers legends such as Paul Gascoigne or Brian Laudrup?"

Ronald de Boer: "Yes, they are probably at my level."

"We are Rangers, Super Rangers, No-One Likes Us, We Don't Care."

Terrace chant first heard in the 1980s which almost hints at some rare self-deprecation

> ❝He was the best young midfielder I had seen. The way he could see runs was just incredible. If it hadn't been for his injury, then Ian would have been one of the best players in the world.❞

Ray Wilkins *on Ian Durrant who retired early through injury*

‟One of the best years of my life was the very last one of my career. Playing for Rangers was my dream and it meant everything to my family. „

Andy Gray *who played at Ibrox in the 1988–89 season*

❛Mr McLeish, you are a magician.❜

A fan to Alex McLeish at the Rangers AGM after
Rangers won the Treble in 1998–99

'We set realistic targets, but when you are at Rangers it is the championship which really matters and rightly so. I felt at the start of the season we have the players to push Celtic and we did exactly that.'

Alex McLeish *on his Treble-winning team*

❝ My family will miss Rangers, maybe more than me. They have said that they'll still be at Ibrox for almost every home game. **❞**

Arthur Numan *on why he will never really leave Rangers*

'The things I won't miss about Rangers? The way the players eat beans before a game. I mean, how can you do that? It's disgusting.'

Arthur Numan

'What kind of player was he? Three goals from 500-odd games.'

Archie Knox *on Walter Smith*

❝F*** off. I've got a pub to run and goats to feed.**❞**

*A semi-retired **Andy Goram** when Sir Alex Ferguson rang to ask him to fill in the United goal. He thought it was a wind-up by Ally McCoist*

❝As that great philosopher Doris Day said, "Que Sera, Sera".**❞**

Alex McLeish *muses after a difficult period at Ibrox*

❝When it sinks in I think I'll probably reflect and say it is the highlight of my career. We have come a long way since August when we were battered by the press. The spirit of the players has been phenomenal.❞

Alex McLeish, *after clinching the title on that dramatic day in May 2005*

❝Every Rangers supporter will recall the events at Easter Road on 22 May 2005 for the rest of their lifetime. This was possibly the most emotionally charged League Championship victory that we have witnessed. Alex and his team deserve enormous credit for the way that they never gave up. **❞**

Chairman **David Murray**, *Chairman's Statement*, Rangers Annual Report 2005

❝I am absolutely jubilant because they played a very disciplined performance tonight against a very dangerous team. The players were magnificent – fantastic. It is a great night for Scottish football and, more importantly, for Rangers.❞

Alex McLeish *celebrates the 1–1 draw with Internazionale which made Rangers the first Scottish club to reach the revamped Champions League knock-out stage*

It's not what you'd want as a player. You want to play in front of 80,000 or 90,000 people. It would have been some experience for the fans as well. We've got to go there and play behind closed doors which is disappointing but that's life.

Barry Ferguson, *previewing Rangers' September 2005 UEFA Champions League trip to Milan when Internazionale's games were played behind closed doors*

❛ We will have to try and get results away from home because it's difficult to play in an empty stadium and you never know what might happen. ❜

Inter coach **Roberto Mancini***, worried about facing Rangers without support in the San Siro*

.I think when the decision was made to leave Rangers, it was a weight off my shoulders and, I think, off the shoulders of those around me.

Alex McLeish, *before his last game as Rangers boss, May 2006*

I think if you can come in with your own team of people and use their expertise along with that which is already in place, then that's the ideal way for me to work.

Paul Le Guen, *happy to select his own backroom staff at Ibrox, May 2006*

When you have someone you feel undermines you, it becomes harder and harder.

Le Guen *decides to strip Barry Ferguson of the captaincy in January 2007*

❝I want to play in every game. I don't want to miss games.**❞**

Barry Ferguson, *after his fall-out with Le Guen*

'Having met with Paul it was clear that in the interests of the club we agreed jointly to him stepping down as manager.'

*Chairman **David Murray** announces*
Le Guen's departure – two days later

❝I am delighted to return to Rangers as manager. This club has always been in my blood and I can't wait to get started.**❞**

Walter Smith, *on his return to Ibrox as manager*

‘It was a privilege to pull on the Rangers jersey for so many years but I am delighted to return as assistant manager.’

Ally McCoist, *on becoming Walter Smith's assistant, January 2007*

‘Different players have different strengths and all I can do when I'm in the team is score and show I'm good enough to play.’

Kris Boyd, *scorer of 52 goals in 61 Rangers SPL starts, but not in the squad for the Champions League*

❛Let's not kid ourselves, Barcelona are one of the best teams on the planet. To be on the same pitch as them and get a point is a great achievement. ❜

Barry Ferguson, *after a 0–0 home draw with Barcelona in the Champions League, October 2007*

"Rangers have done well so far, beating Stuttgart and beating Lyon so I see no reason why they cannot qualify."

Barcelona's **Thierry Henry** *backs Rangers for the knock-out stages of the 2008 Champions League*

It was a day when the most committed atheist might believe in miracles.

Stephen Halliday, The Scotsman,
after Rangers had won the title in 2005